Introducing Reflective Learning

*Prepared for the course team
by Caroline Ramsey*

OU Business School

The course team

Caroline Ramsey (*Course Team Chair and Author*)

Emir Forken (*Course Manager*)

Jeanne Barby (*Course Team Assistant*)

Colin Stanton (*Course Team Assistant*)

Louise Barton (*Programme Co-ordinator*)

Pandy Brodie (*External Assessor and Examiner*)

Donna Gallagher (*Critical Reader*)

Morag Harvey (*Work-based Learning Adviser*)

Jonathan Hughes (*Author*)

Mike Lucas (*Author*)

Lesley Messer (*Programme Manager*)

Pam Shakespeare (*Critical Reader*)

Jane Smith-Bodden (*Critical Reader*)

George Watson (*Regional Manager*)

Course production

Simon Ashby (*Editor*)

Paul Beeby (*Media Project Manager*)

Holly Clements (*Media Assistant*)

Lene Connolly (*Print Buyer*)

Howard Davies (*Interactive Media Developer*)

Jonathan Davies (*Designer*)

Diane Hopwood (*Media Assistant*)

Lisa Osbourne (*Service Administrator*)

Jon Owen (*Graphic Artist*)

Dave Pilgrim (*Interactive Media Developer*)

Kelvin Street (*Learning and Teaching Librarian*)

First published 2006. Second edition 2007.

Edited and designed by The Open University.

Typeset by Pam Callow, S&P Enterprises (rfod) Ltd.

Printed in the United Kingdom by The Charlesworth Group, Wakefield

ISBN 978 0 7492 2723 4

2.1

Contents

What is 'reflective learning'?

I was talking to a friend yesterday and he asked me what I was planning to do over the weekend. 'Oh,' I said, 'I've got to write a booklet on reflective learning.' Richard gave me a quizzical look and asked me what that was. I wonder if, when you picked up this book, you asked the same question. For some people, the idea of reflecting upon what you have done and thinking about how you could do better next time will seem a natural activity. And yet there is more to reflective learning than that, so it is important to spend a short time at the start of this booklet thinking about what a regular, thoughtful practice of reflecting on how we do our jobs, live in a family or relate with others might include. To start this process, have a look now at Activity 1.

Activity 1
*Allow **5 minutes***

Can you think of an occasion that had a major effect on you? Pause for a moment or two and then write down what happened and how you feel you changed as a result.

Comment

Did you find that easy or difficult to do? I remembered an incident about a year ago. I had always enjoyed teaching undergraduate management classes but a project had taken me away for a couple of years to work with managers in a major engineering company. So, last September, I found myself back in a classroom again, teaching management theory to young undergraduates who did not have any work experience. This time I found it very difficult to work just with book theory; I wanted to work with managers who had particular issues that they had to deal with and use my knowledge of management theory to help them. You see, I had changed over the two years, and what once was interesting and enjoyable had palled. I also realised that I was more and more interested in research and reflective learning. It was time to change jobs.

One strange thing about that experience was that I didn't realise what was happening at the time. It took a few weeks for me to notice something was different and then I stopped and thought about it for a few minutes, trying to work out what was going on.

At its very simplest, reflective learning is a deliberate process of undertaking what we will call *cycles of inquiry*. The term 'cycle' is used to capture the way a reflective learner moves between action and reflection. As you can see from the diagram below, there is a sense in which taking action will result in our doing things differently and we can then reflect on what happened next. The reflection should lead to action and so we 'cycle' between action and reflection.

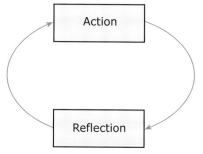

Figure 1   The action–reflection cycle

A key word here is 'deliberate'. I'm sure that at some time or other we have thought about what we have just done and wondered how else we could have acted. It is a somewhat different process, however, to set about improving our work or life performance on purpose by actively considering how we should act, then designing and carrying out a new action before stepping back to consider if the new action has made a difference. This, then, is when everyday reflection becomes a serious practice of learning. This is when we can change the way we live and work.

Tom's story

I guess that I'm not very different to any stepdad. I just struggled getting along with my wife's eight-year-old daughter. It didn't matter what I tried, I was always compared unfavourably with her dad and very clearly given the message that I wasn't her 'real' dad. This was especially the case whenever I tried to bring some discipline into our lives. I thought long and hard about how I could improve the situation, how I could show Amy that I was on her side – that I wanted us to create our own relationship not a replacement 'dad' relationship.

I knew that Amy was very keen on nature and so one weekend I suggested that we went to the local nature reserve. Slightly reluctantly, Amy agreed. I did a whole load of searching on the web to find out about the place before we went. The day wasn't a complete disaster – we had some good times but I guess that Amy could see right through me. Nature really isn't my thing; I'm an engineer.

I thought about it a bit more. Somehow, it seemed to me, I had to find a way of creating a relationship that didn't imitate what Amy thought of as her relationship with her dad. I wasn't sure what to do but I decided to look out for opportunities. Actually, I didn't have to wait long. A week or so later, Amy and I were watching a news programme about global warming and energy use. In particular, it mentioned that fitting valves onto individual radiators could save a large amount of energy. Amy was pretty keen on this; apparently her class had discussed it in a recent science lesson. So, I asked her what she knew about it and whether it was something we could do at home. She disappeared upstairs to her room and brought down her school notes. We talked about it for a while and I asked if she would help me sort out our central heating. The next weekend we set off together to the DIY shop, Amy giving me some 'advice' as to what to buy and acting as my plumber's mate, with me using my plumbing skills to change all the radiators.

Was this a breakthrough for Amy and me? I don't know, but it was a good day, when we enjoyed being with each other and doing something together.

Activity 2

Allow
10 minutes

Tom's is such an ordinary story; I suspect that many of us have been in similar situations. I wonder, however, how many of us would have thought that we were doing some learning then – we tend to pass through such tricky times and put it down to experience. Well, this type of experience can be a source of learning.

1   I mentioned above about going through cycles of inquiry, where action is followed by reflection. Can you see in Tom's story two cycles of inquiry? Note down Tom's two actions and two reflections.

2   Now, think back to a time when you have done something similar either at work or at home.

3   Finally, think of some current situation where some deliberate reflective work might be helpful.

Comment

Tom's first cycle of inquiry was when he considered how to do something with Amy that she would enjoy. The action was to take her to a nature reserve. This outing led to further reflection as Tom realised that this action had not created the hoped-for improvement in relations. The outcome of this reflection was the aim of finding some shared activity that wouldn't mean that Amy compared him unfavourably with her father. The action from this reflection was not so obvious: Tom chose to look out for opportunities to do something new, something that would work for them.

It is worth making a couple of points here which I will return to later on. First, notice Tom's aim to look out for new opportunities. An important part of reflective learning is a growing awareness of what is going on around you. Second, notice how Tom had to wait for an opportunity. We don't control everything and so, as you will see in the section called 'Including others in our reflection', we have to learn how to be aware of the impact of others on our actions.

Creating new actions through thinking reflectively

If one important aspect of reflective learning is that it is deliberate, then a second, and related, aspect is that it is focused on the future. It's all very well looking back on an event and wishing that we had acted differently or saying, 'If that happened again, I'd act differently.' We all know that things never happen the same way twice! So, for learning to happen, you need to use your thinking to affect future actions. The three points you need to consider are:

• generating and evaluating new ideas

• reflecting upon events and situations

• reflecting upon relations.

Generating and evaluating new ideas

This is an important point. Too often managers in organisations, when faced with difficult problems, resort to 'just trying harder'. A crucial part of learning is doing things differently and being able to evaluate the success of these new practices. This point takes us back to my earlier comment about reflective learning being a deliberate practice, with a conscious decision about testing our learning through cycles of inquiry. So, how can you generate new ideas? How can you handle those ideas in order to use them for your learning? One source of new ideas is reading books or thoughtful articles. Not everyone finds reading, especially academic books, easy. I suspect that is because, especially when it has involved reading for learning, we have tended to try and memorise what we read. That makes reading a really hard graft. However, when you read with your eye on how you do your job, then you are not looking to understand every detail; you are looking out for what strikes you, what moves you or what intrigues you. You are looking for possibilities, for ideas that might just work in your life.

Activity 3

*Allow **15 minutes**, with a few days to put the idea into practice*

1   Go back over the first few pages of this booklet and see if you can find one suggestion that might offer you a way of doing things differently at work. Make a note of it here.

2   Now think of when you could make this change and how you would know if it had been helpful or not.

Comment

Well done – you have successfully set up your first cycle of inquiry!

There are other ways of getting ideas – from television programmes, conversations or even just going out for a walk. Sometimes we have to avoid being efficient in order to learn! We all need space to think and wonder and that sort of space is often in very short supply, so you will have to make it for yourself.

Reflecting upon events and situations

I'll be dealing with this topic in much greater depth in the remainder of this booklet. It is important to mention here that time is a major issue in reflective learning. We need to make time to consider what has happened and what we can learn from it to shape our own future actions.

Reflecting upon relations

Sometimes we tend to consider only our own actions and think about what difference they might make. However, I would suggest that even when we are trying to do something on our own, the actions of others will limit or help what we are trying to do. Relations, therefore, are crucially important and paying attention to how they develop is a vital reflective skill. I will return to this in more detail later.

What do we reflect on?

So what will be the object of our reflection? How can we put frames around parts of our lives so that we can consider them more carefully?

Frames

You will see this term quite frequently throughout this booklet. 'Framing' is the act of putting boundaries around events or thoughts to give them a clear focus. For example, you might watch a tennis match and frame it in different ways: you might focus on how to play a backhand shot, or on how to play at the net, or on how to be an umpire. Depending on how you frame the match, you will see very different things.

Framing can be very important to how we learn reflectively as it will determine what we can learn and what events we are likely to notice.

For our purposes, I will suggest three possibilities:

- critical incidents
- a period of time
- an ongoing issue as a focus of inquiry.

Critical incidents

Sensitise: this is a process of being more aware of what's going on around us or being sensitive to the possible importance of those events.

These are situations or events that are, in some way, memorable and significant to us. In particular, look out for incidents where your assumptions about people or the world are challenged or where your current way of working appears to be less than effective. Pay attention to any feelings that something is not quite right, but don't just look for problems: notice the occasions when you catch yourself saying 'if only...' or the times when you feel that if you could do 'that' then you could also do something else. Whatever the prompt, you need to sensitise yourself to the feeling or thought that an event or situation is worth considering at greater length.

Activity 4

Allow
8 minutes

Jot down some possible 'critical incidents' from your home or working life over the last month.

Comment

Use the information above to help remind you what would indicate a critical incident. Think especially of those times when you thought 'if only...' or where you thought that you could do better next time.

Critical incidents are probably the most common form of reflective learning and you will notice that at least two of the reflective frameworks I introduce later will use critical incidents. The benefit is that critical incidents can provide a clear time boundary around events and a clear focus on a topic of learning. This, however, can also be its weakness as sometimes those boundaries become blinkers.

A period of time

Many people keep a journal of some sort and so reflect back upon how the day or week has gone. Doing this sort of regular reflection can often help us note and give time to consider critical incidents that happen during the day. For me, I find that keeping a journal helps me notice themes and issues that are important to me but which are like undercurrents that I don't notice until I read back on a few days' journal entries and see them coming up. In this way, I can counter the problem of blinkers that I noted in the Comment to Activity 4.

Activity 5

Allow
5 minutes

....

Do you have any experiences of keeping a journal or diary? When have you used them and how useful have they been?

Comment   ....

So, are your experiences of keeping a journal positive? I must admit that I sometimes find them difficult to maintain but I'm always aware of the benefits when I do keep a journal. That's especially the case when I keep a journal to track my inquiry into a particular topic focus. We will look at this form of reflective thinking next.

An ongoing issue as a focus of inquiry

Here the focus of your reflection will be on some issue that is of importance to you. Some examples could include improving working relations with another department, improving the quality of a customer service or improving the ways you handle difficult customers. It could be something from your home life. For me recently, one of my focuses of inquiry has been my weight. So I've been looking at what I eat, when I eat and how I could change my eating habits. I've kept a journal noting when I've been successful or not. This is a long-term inquiry for me, and it will need several cycles of inquiry to start making a difference.

Activity 6

Allow
8 minutes

....

Can you think of any focuses of inquiry that are important to you?

Comment   ....

The key benefit of this process is that it allows you to choose your focus and make sure that it is one of significant importance to you. This focus then becomes the basis for you to design a series of cycles of inquiry with an aim of improving your professional or life practice. We will talk about this more in the final section of this booklet.

Now, of course, it is important to state that none of these frames is exclusive. It is very likely that as you focus on one area of learning for this course, you will notice and reflect on several critical incidents and you might well benefit from keeping a regular journal, if not daily then weekly.

Why develop your reflective skills?

Before we move on to the practice of reflective learning, I want to pause for a moment. I wonder if some of you reading this booklet are saying to yourselves, 'But I do this already!' We can have a sense that reflective learning is just common sense and something that we do as a natural activity during our day-to-day lives. Well, that may be true, but I would suggest that there are three important reasons for trying to develop your reflective skills beyond what you do already:

1   I would want to re-emphasise the deliberateness of reflective learning. This isn't something that is done naturally, but is something that we consciously focus on in order to improve some aspect of our lives. In undertaking reflective learning, we are

deliberately seeking to change our lives and world. This is serious stuff and can be incredibly exciting!

2   Common sense can be a dangerous thing. It is rarely sensible and almost never common! Often I find that using someone else's methods helps me to notice some important point that I hadn't noticed before. The very fact that it isn't natural is what helps sensitise me to important issues and stops me being blinkered.

3   Careful reflective learning can make some of our assumptions more explicit. Have you ever noticed, when looking back on some situation that went wrong, how often the word 'assume' comes into your description? Try it and see. You might have assumed that a colleague would be at a meeting, that they would do a particular task, or that everyone would know about the report you wrote last year. It can be a crucial piece of our learning jigsaw as we make explicit the different factors that are shaping our actions. It can be quite illuminating when we stop and consider what it was that we believed we 'didn't need to think about' because it was so obvious. Our assumptions can be a very dangerous block to learning.

We are now ready to go on to a more detailed description of three methods of reflective learning. There are many more methods, of course, and you will find some recommendations for further reading on page 36. The important point is not to seek out some 'correct' form of reflective learning, but to seek out a method that works for you.

Frameworks for reflective learning

Having introduced the general idea of reflective learning, we will now move on to look at three frameworks for reflecting. Frameworks can be very helpful in pointing us to what issues we should consider and can also help us to be thorough in our reflection.

> **Frameworks**
>
> Frameworks offer a structured way of breaking up larger activities. So we might notice that we think about our experiences but we probably wouldn't get into more detail than that. A framework, such as Kolb's learning cycle that I discuss below, is a way of breaking that 'thinking about' into distinct activities that follow logically on from each other.

Having said that, you should still use the frameworks below as guides rather than rules or techniques. To begin with I would recommend that you stay fairly close to one or other of these frameworks, then, as you get more experienced, try to use the parts that work for you in conjunction with elements from other reflective frameworks.

A very common visual tool for reflective frameworks is the use of a cycle or spiral. The idea is that at the end of your reflective learning you will take some action. Consequently, this action will lead to new situations for you to reflect upon and so the cycle starts again. I really want to emphasise the idea that good reflective learning involves action, trying out new ideas or testing new ways of acting. It is just too easy to think about something, come up with some good ideas and then do nothing. One way to think about this is to say that reflective learning is not a process of learning *about*; it is more a process of learning *what* and *how* to act.

Kolb's experiential learning cycle

First, we'll look at Kolb's learning cycle, which is probably the most frequently taught model of experiential, reflective learning.

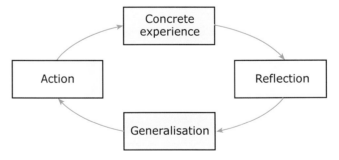

Figure 2   Kolb's experiential learning cycle (adapted from Kolb, 1984)

A concrete experience

If you were using Kolb's cycle, you would start with an actual experience, a sequence of events or some situation; something that you would consider a critical incident. This involves giving very careful attention to an accurate retelling of what happened, trying very hard not to edit out those elements of an event or situation that are uncomfortable to recall. When journalists are getting a story they are encouraged to answer the following questions: who, what, where, when, why and how. If you adopt this approach, the first four questions will help you sort out what happened and the final two questions will help with the next stage of reflection.

Activity 7

Allow
30 minutes

Go back to the event that you thought of during Activity 1 and use the first four questions to help you describe what happened.

Exercise 1

Who was there, who were the active participants, who said what, who was listening, who was less involved?

Comment

Do work hard to remember everyone present, even those only slightly involved. Sometimes it's easy to stop at the main 'actors'. It can be surprising just how important some people can be just by being present, and sometimes the fact that a particular person didn't do anything can be highly significant.

Exercise 2

What was the sequence of events?

Comment

Try to visualise the occasion or occasions. For example, it can be very important to notice if an event happened before or after a particular person entered a room or if it happened before or after something else was said or done. Also, be very careful in your description of what actually happened. 'Concrete experience' can be a difficult concept, as it is hard to be truly objective about what happened. We all tend to see things happening from our own perspective. So one thing you could do would be to ask someone else who was involved what they thought had happened.

Exercise 3

Where did all this happen?

Comment

At one level this is an obvious and simple question, but be careful: sometimes people can behave very differently during a conversation in a corridor than in a formal meeting in the director's office! So take time to note down where events happened and question, during your reflection, whether this was significant.

Exercise 4

When did things happen?

Comment

This can be linked to the sequence of events but it also includes times of day. For example, did your colleague get angry just because of bad work from the team or because it was the end of the day and she had had a particularly trying meeting during the afternoon?

Well, how different is your account of what happened this time? Is it more detailed? Do you think that you've added some details that might be quite important to your thinking about why things happened as they did?

Have you noticed how, with several of these questions, we have already hinted at reflecting upon the events? In part, you are already thinking through the question 'why', and this is important because your answering of that question will be much easier the more detail you include in your description of a sequence of events or situation that you are reflecting upon.

To help us understand each stage of Kolb's learning cycle, we'll look at Mary's story. As we go through the stages of Kolb's cycle I'll discuss some of the 'mental tools' that you can use to make the most of your reflective learning.

Mary's story

It was a fearful row. To be honest, Bill had suggested that I waited until the next day to talk with our Regional Manager (RM) about the loss of the McIntosh account. 'He's been in the Regional Managers' meeting all day and you know he always comes out of that drained and fed up,' Bill had said.

But I had thought it important that I got back to the agents that evening so that, perhaps, they could do something to save the situation. The RM exploded when I gave him the news, his tea mug flew across the room. 'I told you not to raise the prices!' he yelled. He was referring back to a meeting where we had discussed pricing policies for the region where McIntosh is based. I had understood his point at the time but pricing decisions are not made solely by Regional Managers like him. They also have to be okayed by the Marketing Manager and the Finance Director, and they were both very clear, when I had met with them in the FD's office, that I had to improve the margins on my accounts. At the time, I had felt that I had little option but to go for a price hike.

The RM went on and on, accusing me of disloyalty and threatening me with dismissal because of our reduced sales in the region. Denise had come in at that stage saying that she didn't think that McIntosh had left us because of the price hike. She mentioned that they had been buying less from us for some time now and wondered if the price issue was only an excuse for stopping selling our product at all. She went on to mention that she had heard rumours that McIntosh were trying to go upmarket, selling only more expensive items. This was like a red rag to a bull for the RM. 'So why didn't you know that Mary? Why do I have to hear that kind of information from Denise? She's the sales administrator for goodness sake!'

I was getting angry by now and feeling that the RM was being unfair. 'Of course Denise gets to hear more than me from the customers, she has daily conversations with them over deliveries and you have expressly instructed me to work exclusively through our agent when it comes to sales activity,' I retorted. Then we went on to discuss representative policies and local agency agreements. We argued about the quality of the agent the RM had appointed – I felt that the agent prevented me from knowing what was really going on with McIntosh. We worried over who else might be changing their product strategy and I made a strong point about the difficulty in finding new customers for low price items when we had to pay agents' commissions and restrict ourselves from doing our own customer visits. It was 7 pm before we finished and went home!

Activity 8

Allow
15 minutes

Go through Mary's description and note down where she answers the questions who, what, where and when.

Comment

Who: Mary, Bill, the RM, Denise, the agents, McIntosh, the Marketing Manager and Finance Director, other customers and potential customers.

What: the loss of the McIntosh account, Bill's conversation with Mary, Mary's decision that she needed to speak to the RM that afternoon, the initial explosion together with the 'mug' incident, the RM's accusations and threats, Denise's contribution, further accusations, Mary's reaction to what she sees as unfairness, the discussion continuing until 7pm.

Where: not absolutely clear, but the row seems to have happened in the sales office. There had been another meeting in the FD's office.

When: the row had happened in the later afternoon following a Regional Managers' meeting. There had also been two earlier meetings: one between Mary, the Marketing Manager and FD, and one between Mary and the RM. It is not clear when these meetings happened. There had also been some conversations between Denise and McIntosh staff, but again it is not clear when and for how long these conversations had been going on.

Did you get everyone and every detail? In particular, I wonder if you included the Marketing Manager and FD, or the existing and potential customers. None of these people were actually present at the row but their importance to what was going on is very clear. What do you think about some of the areas of doubt? Particularly interesting to me is the question about when and for how long Denise had been hearing these rumours. I think that if I were Mary, I would go and ask Denise these questions.

Reflection

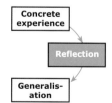

We move on now to the second stage of Kolb's learning cycle. At this stage we are interested in finding out what the really significant actions and words were and we will be answering the questions 'why' and 'how' did these things happen. We will also look at another reflective question that I find very helpful, 'so what?'

To help us work through this reflection stage we will continue to use Mary's story and see how you can look for evidence and build an understanding of what happened in the series of events that Mary is reflecting upon. Remember, the key point is not just to understand what happened but to work from that understanding towards action. I've mentioned it before but it bears repeating: reflective learning is about action!

The first task you have to do is to *frame* the issue that you are trying to deal with. As you saw earlier, framing is a process by which you put boundaries around a topic. It provides you with a way of looking at an issue. Often, as you look at an event, you can frame it in several different ways. One way that you can frame your reflection is by asking the question 'what do I want to change?' If there is nothing in need of change, then you don't have a critical incident and you really don't need to spend too much time considering things. However, the very fact that you have gone to the effort of describing a sequence of events suggests that something has gone awry or that you have a sense that those events could offer a positive area for improvement. Looking at how to frame the events Mary described will explain how to frame a reflection.

Activity 9
Allow
10 minutes

Take a few minutes to list the sorts of question that Mary might have been thinking about as she wrote that description of her experience with the Regional Manager.

Comment

The questions (frames) I came up with can be found in Figure 3 below.

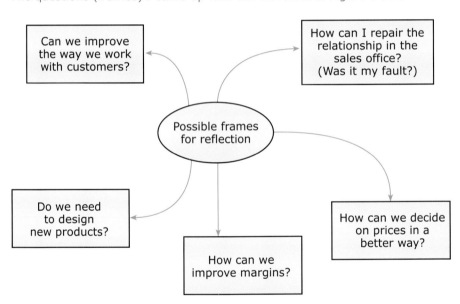

Figure 3   A mind map of possible frames for reflection

Any of these questions could provide a frame that would, in turn, shape Mary's reflection. Answers to the question 'why' would be very different depending on which frame she decided to use. Let's take two frames and see what evidence we come up with from Mary's description. We'll use 'How can I repair the relationship in the sales office?' and 'Can we improve the way we work with customers?' We'll make a table and use phrases from the description to remind us of relevant points.

Do you see how the important points for each way of framing the reflection are different? This is why it is vitally important that you think hard about how to frame your reflection.

Office relations	Customer relations
The RM 'drained and fed up'	Denise in daily contact with customers
'Accusing me of disloyalty'	Is the agent getting in the way?
Sales price decision mechanism	Is the agent good enough?
Denise knowing more than Mary	Cost of the agent's commission
Unfairness of RM	Complexity of pricing decisions
Appointment of agent	

Another point that you will need to consider is what timeframe to work with? For example, when looking at the office relations frame, we can see that Denise's comments caused Mary some problems in that particular row with her manager. What we don't know is whether Denise was actually trying to be helpful or if she had a history of trying to 'score points' off Mary. So Mary would have to think back to see if there were other situations when Denise tried to make things difficult, or if they have a good relationship. The concrete experience–reflection stages of Kolb's cycle are iterative. By that, I mean you may well find that, as you get underway with your reflection, you have to add to your description by thinking back or considering different events. It can be something of a snare within the critical incident method of reflection that one event can blind you to the importance of other, related events, so be careful to avoid this. Using different frames can be a help here. While you are reflecting, try to look at an event from different perspectives.

Activity 10
Allow
10 minutes

For the moment, we're going to look more carefully at the 'office relations' frame. How would you judge the important factors? Think about the situation as Mary describes it. What questions come to the fore? What issues would you take time to consider at greater length?

Comment

So there we have Mary reflecting upon office relations; why did a piece of bad news cause a major row? Several questions arise out of Mary's description. First, there is the simple question of whether she got the RM at a bad moment; that would probably be Bill's evaluation of the affair. Second, it seems to me that there is an issue about pricing. From Mary's description, it seems that the RM was not involved in the final price decision for the McIntosh contract. Now that seems a slightly strange situation to me. Could it have contributed to the RM feeling that others were damaging his authority? That seems to be confirmed by his accusation that Mary is disloyal. Mary would have to work through these and other questions. For example, towards the end of Mary's account the conversation, whilst still heated, seemed to move away from personal issues and get on to important areas of policy where there are significant differences between Mary and her manager.

The many different points discussed here illustrate the importance of framing. It would be all too easy for Mary to focus on how bruised she felt and how unfairly she was treated but there seem to me to be other issues that lie below the surface of the row and they may be more important. This is a crucial aspect of the reflection stage. Don't go straight for the most obvious point but give yourself time to consider alternative causes. So far, I have focused on asking 'why' did things happen the way they did. However, you should not forget to seek answers to the question of 'how' something occurred. The important point here is to notice how a situation built up. It's very rare for there to be just one cause of any human activity and thinking through the moment-by-moment way a situation emerged can indicate other important factors that affected what happened.

Generalisation

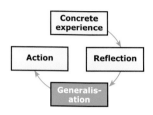

In the third stage of Kolb's learning cycle, you will try to work out what learning you can take from your reflection and apply in other situations. The key question that you will want to answer here is 'so what?' In going through the concrete experience and reflection stages you have, in effect, revealed 'what' happened, so now you need to work out what should be the impact of those events on your future actions. You're asking 'so what?' Later you will need to ask 'now what?' I've taken these questions from Melanie Jasper's (2003) use of earlier reflective work by Borton and you might find those three questions are quite helpful to use alongside Kolb's ideas.

As you try to generalise aspects of your experience your goal will be to identify those aspects of a critical incident that are likely to be significant to your future actions. To do this you could ask questions under the following four headings:

- consistency
- content
- concepts
- consequences.

Let's explore each of these headings a bit, using Mary's story as an example, especially the issue of how her company manages customer relations.

Consistency

First, we can ask questions of *consistency*; things will always happen that are specific to a situation and won't apply to any other situation. For example, take Denise's contribution to Mary's row with the Regional Manager and assume that Mary and Denise are good colleagues who work well together. Considering this information, we would say that Denise's comment caused Mary problems *in that moment only* and that there is no general principle that Mary should consider for future work with Denise. However, I would suggest that the issue of the Marketing Manager and the Finance Director getting involved in pricing decisions might well be a long-term issue that Mary should consider carefully. So, the generalisation stage – sometimes called the theorising stage – is the period when you consider the longer term implications of what happened and when you try to understand where there are consistencies or patterns to certain events and trends that will affect future actions. Here are some questions that may help you:

1   Were the events ongoing or temporary? An issue here might be the involvement of the Marketing Manager and the Finance Director in pricing decisions. Was this an unfortunate, one-off event or is this a common experience?

2   Were the events central to or on the fringe of what happened? Now we want to work out whether events or situations are at the heart of what happened or just part of the surroundings. In Mary's case, the role of the agent is an example. Remember that Mary told the RM that the agent got in the way of her knowing what McIntosh were doing or wanting. Now this might just have been a quick defence that Mary put up to deflect the criticism of her not knowing about the rumours about McIntosh's change in policy or it might well be a central complaint that had been festering for some time. If it is just a defence then the issue of agents is not likely to be a persistent one.

3   Do the events point to something that is deep or superficial? In a way this is similar to the question of centrality but asking a similar question in a different way can often be helpful to reflective learning. I would suggest that the fact that the Regional Manager was tired after a long meeting was a superficial cause of the row. Maybe Mary was unwise to talk to him then, but I suspect that apart from leaving a bad taste in the mouth it wasn't going to have a long-term effect on the department. However, the question about McIntosh changing their own selling strategy might well be very important, especially if other customers followed their example!

Content

Having asked questions about consistency, you now need to ask questions about the *content* of what happened and the people involved. Here you'll need to focus on what the events tell you about yourself, the other people involved and the problems that you are all facing.

Activity 11

Allow **10 minutes**

So, what can you learn from Mary's story about the people involved in relations with customers? You're probably feeling a bit short of information here. Again, notice how the processes of reflection and generalisation keep sending you back to the events with further questions that will affect your description. So what would your questions be? What sort of things do you think could be important to your reflection?

Go back to Mary's story and make a list of questions.

Comment

Well, did you find that an easy task? As is so often the case with reflection, the skill is to be able to separate the significant elements from those that are of passing interest. I'll look at just two possible questions (there are always more you could ask):

1   I'm quite interested in whether the Regional Manager is under pressure. Do you notice how he has been overruled on the pricing issue? Additionally, he seems to find meetings very difficult at the moment. If he were to leave, would his policy of using agents go with him?

2   I'm interested in the agents. Are they really obstructive? Do they really block the flow of important information to Mary? How high is their commission; does it make a significant difference to the products' price?

Mary may well have the answers to these questions but, of course, there is always a problem with bias. How easy do you think that it would be for Mary to admit to herself that she might be as much of the problem as the agent?

It's very difficult to be honestly critical of yourself without going overboard and always taking the blame. This is a skill that can be learned and it is an area where involving trusted friends and colleagues can help. We'll look in more detail at that in a later section.

Concepts

Two more questions will help you to theorise about what caused things to happen and generalise them into advice for the future. First, you need to look at the *concepts* that lay behind your actions. It seems that apparently daft actions often have good reasons lurking behind them! We usually have good reasons for what we do. However, what seemed a good reason at the time could be mistaken; reasoning can be built on faulty or irrelevant information or unchallenged assumptions. For example, do you think that Mary was right to speak with the Regional Manager when she did? Couldn't she have waited until the next morning? She had a sensible reason for talking with him that evening but was she wise to do so? Our actions can often be affected by 'concepts' or 'theories', commonsense, everyday theories like 'tired people can be irritable' or 'our customers are king'. It is always worth questioning the theories, assumptions or reasons that lie behind our actions.

Consequences

Second, we need to spend some time considering the *consequences* for you of what happened. These consequences largely fall into two categories: changes that you will need to make, or changes that you will need to persuade others to make. These questions take us straight into the final stage of Kolb's learning cycle, where we consider actions. But before we get there let's take a moment or two to pause.

Taking a breather!

Are you starting to get the feeling that this reflection thing is complicated? Perhaps you are wondering how anyone would get anything done if they went through all these stages every time anything happened. I wonder how many of you have thought the phrase 'analysis paralysis' as you read the last few pages. Perhaps you have thought that if you did all the analysing and thinking I've suggested, you wouldn't get anything done! There are a few points to make here:

- Yes, good reflection does take time but no, you are not going to do this kind of careful analysis for every situation. You will need to make a decision as to whether the importance of an incident merits the time to think it through carefully. It is not the practice of reflective learning that deserves time, but instead the complex situations that we have to work through that will, on occasion, merit setting some time aside to reflect upon. Our families, job and careers are important to us and if we are thoughtful, we can make a significant difference to how they prosper. Reflective learning isn't the answer to every problem but it can help.

- You do get more skilled at this and many of the questions will come to you as second nature as you get more practiced. Sometimes you'll find yourself just thinking through some of these questions as you drive somewhere or go for a walk. As you get used to reflecting on experience, you will find that it comes more easily and quickly to you.

- You will hopefully find it immensely exciting and rewarding as you gain greater influence over how you live and work!

THINKING OUTSIDE THE SQUARE

Action

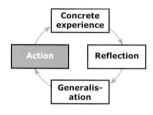

Let's get back to Kolb's reflective learning cycle. Towards the end of the generalisation stage I suggested that you consider what the consequences were for you of the events you were reflecting on. I asked you to think what you would change or what you would work towards changing.

Well, the action stage is...

...when you get on with it!

Don't just think about it, don't just be wise after the event, don't just grumble: get on with making a difference.

That's all there is to this stage really!

There is a little more to say, but the real message I want you to take from this section is to get on with it and take action.

There are just two questions that you need to ask yourself as you take action:

* What do I want and what do I think I can achieve?
* How will I know that I'm on the way?

A few years ago, a friend of mine who worked in the logistics industry was helping me to think through a tricky work situation. I'd worked out what the important problems were and I was trying to plan what to do next. Paul asked me, 'What would "good" look like?' I found that a very helpful question. It might not be good English grammar but it helped me think through what I could realistically aim to do. More recently I have been working with a large engineering company, trying to help them improve their management of new product design and development. There were some big issues that I thought were hampering their work but I knew that these issues were under the control of the parent company. There was simply no way that I would be able to make these changes. So, I looked at areas of management where I could influence people and that's where I put my effort. I had decided what 'good' looked like.

Activity 12

Allow
10 minutes

Think of a tricky work or life situation that you have experienced. Can you think of how you could have applied these two questions to help guide your actions?

Comment

The crucial thing here is to think about what you are trying to achieve – about what is 'desirable'. However, it is not always possible to get everything you want, and so you might need to consider what is feasible – what's the best you can do in the circumstances? Try to be specific in setting objectives and have a clear idea of how you will know that you have been successful. Finally, especially where the learning cycle is likely to last a long time (more than two weeks, perhaps), try to pick out some events that might indicate whether or not your objective is becoming more achievable.

My hobby is sailing dinghies. On the sails of my boat are little bits of fabric called tell-tales. One of the ways that I can know if I'm sailing well is when those tell-tales are streaming out horizontally backwards. If they start drooping down then I know that I have to adjust the tiller. Well, as you look to take action following reflection, you should try and think of what the 'tell-tales' might be for what you're planning to do. How will you know, quickly, that your action is having the desired effect? What events would encourage you that things are going well; what events might cause you to reconsider what you are doing?

So, with those two questions in mind to help guide your action, you can get on with it!

Bringing our feelings into our reflection

Kolb's learning cycle is a very rational model of how we learn. We are expected to try to be as objective as we can so that we can build up theories of why things happen. I don't know about you but I find life to be messier than that! Thoughts and behaviour aren't always rational. Now, of course, a key part of reflective learning is to help us become more thoughtful and less impulsive in our actions, but we do need to include our feelings and their effect on our actions in our reflection. The second framework that I want to introduce to you is helpful in this respect. I've taken it from a book by Mike Pedlar, John Burgoyne and Tom Boydell (2001), who are very well know for their work in helping managers to develop their skills.

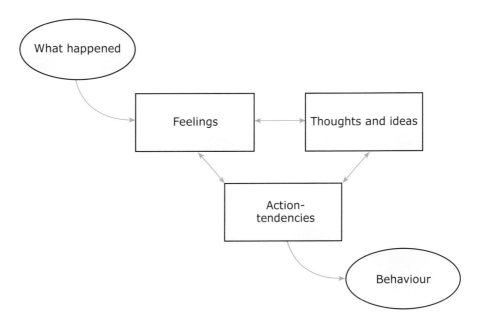

Figure 4   Bringing our feelings into our reflection (Pedlar et al., 2001)

This framework focuses on our response to events that happen around us. It asks us to consider why we acted as we did in particular circumstances and if there might be better ways of acting. As such, Pedlar and his colleagues recommended it as more of a long-term 'journalling' method rather than a one-off reflection on a particular event. In the final section of this booklet, I will write more about journals and learning logs, but for now let's just look at this framework to see what it might add to our reflective skills. There are three components involved in this reflection:

- our feelings
- our thoughts and ideas
- our action-tendencies.

As before, we'll go through them now in a little more detail:

Feelings

Especially in the West, the ability to be rational is highly prized. I won't argue with that idea here but it does have one significant negative effect. Too often we play down the importance of our emotions and feelings especially as they affect our actions. It really doesn't seem too surprising that feelings of dislike for a person, moral outrage at a course of action or fear about our ability to do a job might affect what we decide to do. We can't like everybody, sometimes other people make us angry and we wouldn't need to learn if we were confident about everything we did! So it's perfectly reasonable to expect that our feelings will affect our actions. The trouble is when, in an attempt to appear rational to ourselves and others around us, we hide those feelings and fail to take them into account.

Activity 13

Allow
8 minutes

Reflect back over the last week or so to any event when your think that a colleague's actions, at least in part, were shaped by his or her feelings. Can you describe the event and the actions that were displayed?

Comment

Of course, this won't have happened to you! You wouldn't let your feelings govern you at work. You have been rational and logical all the time...

... or have you?

What sort of feelings are we likely to have in a work situation? Well, the whole range. Have you ever felt:

- jealous of another person's success?
- left out of an important meeting or project?
- encouraged by your boss's praise?
- disheartened by difficulties?
- fearful of a new job?
- excited by a new project?
- intimidated by a senior colleague?

I'm sure you can add to this list; they're part of what it means to be at work or in any of life's difficult situations. They often play a significant role in how we act, so take a little time to consider them. It's not that feelings will always lead to bad actions; it's more that we need to appreciate just how we were feeling in the particular situation that we are reflecting on, in order to fully understand why we acted in the way we did.

Thoughts and ideas

The thoughts and ideas element is similar to the stages of reflection and generalisation in Kolb's learning cycle, but this time you need to think back to remember how you understood a particular situation at the time and ask questions about how you were making sense of the situation as you responded.

Jack's story

I've just been in a meeting with Chris and some of the junior engineers and I'm not happy with the way it went. Actually, if I'm honest, I'm not happy with the way I handled the situation. We're coming up to a major validation event and we're slipping behind our schedule. Chris came into our office wearing his 'I'm the Senior-Project-Manager-and-member-of-the-senior-management-team' hat. I know him when he's in that mood; he won't take no for an answer and he won't listen to any explanation longer than three words. Usually all he wants to hear is 'Yes, Chris, I'll do that right away.' It's not entirely Chris's fault, I guess that it's as much about the macho culture we have here, but it can be impossible to have a reasonable conversation.

Well, by and large, when Chris is in that sort of a mood I just keep quiet, nod my head as though I understand and use a form of words that will keep him happy but without quite committing to anything. Actually, I've become quite skilled at it! It usually works, or at least it delays the inevitable storm, but today there were three young engineers involved and one of them, Deepak, started to explain why what Chris wanted was impossible. Chris went into bulldozer mode; I sensed danger and tried to indicate to Deepak to back off. However, he went on in great engineering detail why Chris's request was impossible. I saw Chris's eyes glaze over before he gave Deepak a clear message about who was boss and exactly where Deepak was located in the company hierarchy. It was pretty unpleasant for the young man. I tried a couple of times to intervene but, if I'm honest, I knew that there was little that I could do to help. You just have to let these things blow over and then pick up the pieces.

Afterwards, I tried to talk it through with Deepak and make some sort of plan but he was very upset and angry with me for not backing him up. In the end, he stormed off. I think that he's at an interview today; we can't afford to lose him, as he's a very promising engineer. I do feel that I let him down but then I'm not sure what I could have done.

I wonder whether you have been in a similar situation. It's sadly all too common for senior managers to bully their subordinates, and it has a longer term effect than just in the moment when it happens.

Activity 14
Allow
5 minutes

Look back at Jack's story and see how previous experience of Chris's behaviour had shaped his thoughts on how to deal with him.

Comment

Notice how Jack's thoughts are also muddled up with his feelings. I suspect that he was feeling pretty uncomfortable during that outburst from Chris, don't you? I think most of us would feel that we wanted to help but would be uncertain of how helpful we could be. Working with other people is difficult and we need time out to reflect and see how we could do things better.

The second part of the thoughts and ideas element is to do with the ideas we had about what we could do. For Jack this centred on waiting for the storm to blow over and then picking up the pieces afterwards. It's worth noting a difference here between Kolb's learning cycle and Pedlar and his colleagues' reflective frame. When Kolb gets to the stage of thinking about action, he's talking there of what action to take next. However, when Pedlar *et al.* ask us to consider our ideas for action, they are referring to the ideas we *had* in a particular situation. The aim of the reflective learning is different. For Pedlar, Burgoyne and Boydell the reflective learning is about understanding how we behave and so giving us a greater chance to improve our performance by noticing those things in our behaviour that might have a negative effect.

Action-tendencies

Action-tendencies are those habitual ways of working that just come out of us. I tend to go for the most radical option available and am usually willing to take on people in authority for an idea that I believe in. I'm not very good at holding back and working out what is feasible and so I tend to put in a great deal of unnecessary work.

Think about your habitual types of action. In a tense situation, what do you tend to do? What is your initial response to difficult requests? Do you tend to want to analyse or get on with some action?

The answers to these questions will be your action-tendencies. Sometimes they will be helpful, but at other times they might get in the way.

Activity 15

Allow
8 minutes

Look back at Jack's story. What do you think that his action-tendencies were? How do you think they might have hindered Jack from taking action in this particular situation?

Comment

Jack tended to back off if Chris was in a bad mood. It appears that there is some thought behind this behaviour, but it could well be a strategy for self-preservation that had become a habit. I wonder if there was a moment in the meeting when Jack could have said to Chris, 'I think Deepak and I need to talk this through and come back to you with a plan', but his tendency toward passivity got in the way of that possibility.

Pedlar and his colleagues are offering a way for you to consider how you behave. They suggest keeping a journal over a period of time so that you can review a series of entries and spot any recurring themes. Are any feelings common? Are any thoughts and ideas consistently helpful or problematic? What are your action-tendencies, and where are they a benefit and where a hindrance? As you consider these points over a sequence of events, so you can seek to modify your behaviour. The benefit of the Pedlar reflective framework seems to be that it allows us to make explicit things that are often tacit or hidden, things like habits, feelings or ways of thinking. The way we act is often a messy affair of rational thought and less considered motivations. Try to make use of these different ideas as you seek constantly to improve your actions and performance in difficult situations.

Including others in our reflection

I think that Kolb's reflective learning cycle is a little weak in a second area. Relationships with other people can affect both what we can do and our actions. Now, you can argue that you can use the second stage of reflection to consider the actions of others but, overall, the cycle is very individualistic – it assumes that we act as independent individuals. Pedlar and his colleagues also talk a great deal about how we, as individuals behave. Anyway, neither of these two reflective frameworks explicitly emphasise how relations affect what we can achieve.

Activity 16
Allow
7 minutes

Look back at Jack's story. Do you think that it would make things clearer if we understood his actions as coming from interactions with Chris rather than just from considering his own feelings? What questions would you ask if you focused more on the way Jack and Chris interacted rather than on Jack's individual actions?

Comment

I wonder if it felt a little strange trying to think about a relationship as one thing. After all, we tend to think about relations as being the result of what two or more individuals do; that's why, I suspect, most reflective frameworks don't mention relations explicitly. However, if we look at the way that the two men interacted, then I think that some new questions arise. For example, why was Chris becoming aggressive? Were there any signs that Chris might not be willing to listen to long explanations? What could Jack have done to defuse a confrontation?

Do you notice that in asking these questions I am asking you to attend to the moment-by-moment way that a situation arose? This is something like the 'how' question that I introduced in the description stage of Kolb's learning cycle. What is important here is what we *attend* to in our actions.

> **Attend**
>
> 'Attending to' is the process by which we 'look out for' or 'focus our attention upon' something. An example is when I advise managers to attend to work conversations rather than just the task in hand.

Judi Marshall (2001) has done some very helpful work in this area and we shall use some her ideas to finish this introduction to reflective learning. Marshall wrote of two attentional disciplines. First, we shall look at *inner arcs of attention*, then *outer arcs of attention* before going on to discuss how we can attend to our involvement in ongoing action. Let's look at each of these arcs of attention in a little more detail. I think that you will notice some themes coming through from earlier discussions, especially as you consider the inner arcs of attention.

Inner arcs of attention

Our inner arcs of attention focus on:

- our assumptions
- our patterns of activity
- our response to others
- the language we use
- the way we make sense of what's going on.

Marshall recommends that we attend to these inner arcs with curiosity and playfulness. This is not something to get terribly introspective about, but to notice and wonder how we could be different, to try out different assumptions or responses.

Outer arcs of attention

In attending to outer arcs we will be noticing:

- what is going on around us
- how we are affecting that
- how we are maintaining or changing a situation
- how we can test our assumptions
- how other people are making sense of the same events or situation.

Activity 17
Allow
10 minutes

Go back to Jack's story. Can you suggest some questions that he might ask himself if he were to use Marshall's framework to help him reflect on what happened?

Comment

I think that Jack might consider the following points:

- Was I really attending to what was going on?
- To what extent was I complicit in Chris's behaviour? To what extent was my passivity an encouragement to him being overbearing?
- More than that, in accepting the current macho-behaviour of senior management, am I actually ensuring that it continues? Is there a sense in which we all get so desensitised to aggressive behaviour that the only way that senior managers can make people aware of the importance of an issue is to become aggressive?
- How can I test my assumptions about the best way of dealing with Chris?
- Who amongst my colleagues could I talk to about this and seek ways to improve the situation?

I would suggest that these are very different to the kinds of question that were coming out of the Kolb or Pedlar *et al.* frameworks. The attentional disciplines are at their best when we learn to use them 'in the moment' rather than at some point after an event takes place. That will take quite a bit of practice, but there are two ways of getting used to them. First, you can use them alongside other reflective methods after a critical incident. Second, some time when you're in a meeting where you don't need to say much, try listening to the discussion using Marshall's inner and outer arcs of attention to frame how you notice your responses to what is going on and how other people behave.

Alongside the two attentional disciplines, Marshall proposed two further frames to help us attend to how we are involved in ongoing action. First, she wrote about consciously cycling between action and reflection. Second, she pointed out that there are times to persist, pursue and shape our world – times to be active – but there are, equally, times when we need to focus on what she calls 'communion'. These are times to focus on relationships with others, on listening and discussing. These are the cycles of inquiry I discussed earlier and the crucial thing about them is that they are active and they involve us in an ongoing inquiry. We will look at them in more detail in the final section.

Starting a self-reflective inquiry

In this final section, I want to do three things:

- I want to discuss how you could organise a serious, ongoing inquiry into some subject that you consider important and where you want to improve your performance.
- I want to discuss the benefits of writing your reflections and keeping a journal or learning log.
- I will suggest one or two ways that you can get others to help you in your reflective learning.

Self-reflective inquiry

Self-reflective inquiry is the name Marshall (2001) gives to the process of undertaking a sustained investigation into professional practice. You will remember that in the first section I suggested that there were three bases for our reflection: a critical incident, a period of time, or a particular learning theme. These are by no means exclusive – indeed I would fully expect that any sustained inquiry into a particular theme, issue or focus of inquiry would be very likely to include many critical incidents and daily or weekly journals. Right now, however, I want to focus on how to set up an inquiry into a theme or issue that is important to your professional practice or your involvement in other aspects of your daily life.

At the heart of any self-reflective inquiry are cycles of inquiry, where action is followed by reflection, which then prompts further action, leading to more reflection and so on. However there are some other important elements that you will need to consider.

Choosing a focus of inquiry

It may seem an obvious point but you need to choose what will be the focus of your self-reflective inquiry. This, however, is often not quite as simple as it might seem.

Activity 18

Allow
30 minutes

There are three points to consider when choosing the focus of an inquiry. Use the advice in the left-hand column to help you answer the questions in the right-hand column.

First, the focus of your inquiry needs to have a strong link with how you actually do your job or act in whatever sphere of life that is important to you. Don't make a focus of inquiry out of something that you'd like to know about. This kind of inquiry is all about action and the professional practice you undertake, so focus on some area of your day-to-day practice with the aim of making a difference to the way you do your job or carry out your life.	Where do you want to change or improve the way you work? Note down one or two options.

Second, the focus of your inquiry should be within your own zone of autonomy, by which I mean your inquiry should be about *your* practice. It isn't worth spending a large amount of time conducting an inquiry into how someone else ought to do their job, although it might be very tempting at times!

In which areas of your work will changing your day-to-day practice make a significant difference?

Finally, consider the scope of your proposed inquiry. Is it manageable? Can you make the time for it?

Are there any particular time restrictions that you may face?

Comment

Your answers to these questions will help you to decide on the focus of your inquiry.

Consciously moving between action and reflection

Marshall suggests two ways of moving between action and reflection:

1   Make clear decisions about the times when you need to persist with some action, when you should pursue a particular goal and when you should seek to shape the circumstances around you. You should *also* be clear about times when you need to pause or discuss with others and allow your actions to be shaped by responsiveness to your circumstances.

2   You should consciously move between times of action when you try out and test new ideas, and times of reflection when you evaluate the success (or otherwise) of that action.

Judging when to end an inquiry

Inquiries can run out of steam and stop you achieving what you want to do. Perhaps a new focus of inquiry crops up that will be more productive and so you move on to that. Then there are also times when you need to pause in an inquiry or notice that your inquiry is becoming a little too focused on yourself and not including working with others. There can be times when you get bogged down in a particular issue and need to step back and regain perspective. Marshall suggests that being consciously playful and curious are helpful here and so is a correct evaluation of yourself. You need to keep a balance between taking yourself seriously enough – your work and career merit careful thought – but also being able to laugh at yourself and so know when to lighten up a little! Judging when to end an inquiry can be very significant to your sense of its long-term benefit.

Writing journals or learning logs

As a general rule of thumb, keeping some written record of your inquiry is very helpful. Many people keep a journal of some sort. You don't have to do it every day but some people really enjoy it, and how you write your reflective learning down really is up to you.

Writing a journal or a learning log?

I ought to start by saying that there isn't a clear definition of which is which, but I generally think of a journal as something that you write on a regular basis, perhaps daily or two or three times per week. A learning log might be written less regularly and is often linked to recording reflections on critical incidents. The danger that I've noticed with learning logs is that people can forget to write down their reflections on a critical incident – it might be a good idea to set aside some time every week for writing about your reflective learning. Journals are not without their problems either, with there being a temptation just to write descriptions of what has happened that day or vague, unstructured musings. If you're new to journalling, do give yourself time to find out what works for you; don't expect to be perfect at it from day one. Writing is a craft that is learned with practice. One of my habits is writing memos to myself. The important point here is to get started!

Writing or typing?

I generally recommend typing and encourage people to learn how to touch-type (it's not that difficult to become reasonably good at it) but I have to confess that I hand write my journal. There's something about pausing, taking time, dwelling on a topic and *not* being too efficient. Which do you find easier? Remember that using a computer can help keep things tidy and allows you to cut and paste bits and pieces or correct mistakes without lots of crossing out. The important point here is to get started! Have I mentioned that before?

What gets written?

Start with a critical incident or two, and then as your inquiry gets underway, write about the cycles of inquiry that you design and carry out. You can also note down significant events or conversations and perhaps include emails, letters or notices you receive. The important point here, as I'm sure you've guessed, is to get started!

Working with others

Sometimes it can be really helpful to get other people's view on your inquiry. This might just be on an informal basis, for example, when checking up on some of our assumptions or memory of an event. However, I would recommend that you consciously choose someone or a group to travel the journey of an inquiry with you. One good idea is to ask someone you respect and who knows about the issues within your focus of inquiry to act as your mentor. By and large it is not a good idea to use your direct line manager, but sometimes that works. Another good idea is to create an Action Learning Set with four or five others who are also undertaking similar inquiries.

An Action Learning Set is a group of between 4 and 6 people who join together to support each other in undertaking reflective learning.

If you do use an Action Learning Set, then you need to arrange either to meet up or exchange correspondence.

If you're able to meet up, one possible format for the meeting is as follows:

> Each member of the Learning Set is given 30 minutes to work through their issues. It's important to prepare for this. Think about which issues you want other people to help you work through.
>
> **10 minutes**
>
> Tell others what's been going on and introduce the topic that you want to talk about. Two points to note here:
>
> 1   The 'presenter' decides what they want to discuss and the other set members (the supporters) accept that.
> 2   The 'supporters' keep quiet and let the presenter talk without interruption.
>
> **10 minutes**
>
> Supporters can ask questions for clarification. Look for things that don't quite add up, things that are surprising or gaps in information. Importantly, ask questions, don't tell the presenter what you would do!
>
> **10 minutes**
>
> Work out what to do next. Here the supporters need to be really careful not to say what they would do but ask questions that will help the presenter to work out what she or he should do. The presenter can help in this by 'thinking out loud' about what they will do next; the supporters can often notice how well that fits with what they have heard in the previous twenty minutes.

If you can't make it to a meeting, the same three stages can easily be conducted by email or other correspondence. If you are able to set up telephone conference calls, then that can also work, but I tend to think that it is quite tricky if you are dealing with sensitive, personal issues.

Concluding words

Well, we've finally got to the end of this introduction to reflective learning. Don't expect to be able to put into practice all the above ideas flawlessly straight away. I can't always carry them out perfectly after several years trying but I do know that they help me to do my job! Give yourself the space to learn and improve in your reflective learning. Keep trying new ideas and notice if they help or get in the way. Finally, if you want to learn how to learn reflectively, there really is only one thing you need to do now...

(I suspect that you know what's coming – but then it's good to be predictable sometimes)

... get started!

References

Argyris, C. and Schön, D. (1978) *Organizational Learning: A Theory of Action Perspective*, Reading, MA, Addison-Wesley.

Jasper, M. (2003) *Beginning Reflective Practice,* Cheltenham, Nelson Thornes.

Kolb, D. (1984) *Experiential Learning*, Englewood Cliffs, NJ, Prentice Hall.

Marshall, J. (2001) 'Self-Reflective Inquiry Practices', in Reason, P. and Bradbury, H. (eds) *Handbook of Action Research*, London, Sage.

Pedlar, M., Burgoyne, J. and Boydell, T. (2001) *A Manager's Guide to Self-Development* (4th edn.), Maidenhead, McGraw-Hill.

Further reading

If this introduction to reflective reading has interested you or if you would like to read more guides to reflection, I would suggest that the following books or articles might be helpful.

Melanie Jasper's book *Beginning Reflective Practice* (2003, Nelson Thornes) is excellent. Its only problem is that its intended audience is trainee nurses and so all the illustrations are to do with healthcare. However, if you can work around that then she introduces other reflective frameworks that you might find helpful. I thought that Chapters 1, 3 and 5 were particularly good.

Mike Pedlar, John Burgoyne and Tom Boydell are very well known for their work on what has been called the learning organisation. Their *Manager's Guide to Self-Development* (2001, McGraw-Hill) is a fascinating collection of exercises that you can do to help you improve your skills as a manager if that is what your work entails.

You might find it difficult to get hold of Judi Marshall's chapter from the *Handbook of Action Research*. If you do have trouble finding it, then you will be able to find a similar article in a journal held in the Open Library electronic journals collection called *Systemic Practice and Action Research*:

Marshall, J. (1999) 'Living life as inquiry', *Systemic Practice and Action Research*, vol. 12, issue 2.

Acknowledgements

Grateful acknowledgement is made to the following sources for permission to reproduce material in this book.

Illustrations

Page 6: © Reg Charity/Corbis

Page 10: © Rainer Raffalski / Alamy;

Page 21: © www.CartoonStock.com;

Page 22: Courtesy of David Hope;